The Adventures of
Copper, the Little Papillon

COPPER GETS ADOPTED

Christine Farmer

innovo PUBLISHING

Published by
Innovo Publishing LLC
www.innovopublishing.com
1-888-546-2111

Providing Full-Service Publishing Services for
Christian Authors, Artists, and Organizations: Hardbacks, Paperbacks,

eBooks, Audiobooks, Music, and Film

COPPER GETS ADOPTED

Library of Congress Control Number: 2014944764
ISBN 13: 978-1-61314-222-6

Cover Design & Interior Layout by Innovo Publishing LLC
Printed in the United States of America
U.S. Printing History
First Edition: July 2014

Dedicated to Marcus and Teresa.
Thank you for bringing Copper into our lives.

Bonjour (hello). Allow me to introduce myself.
My name is Copper, and I am a little Papillon.
That means "butterfly" in French.
See my ears? They are shaped like a butterfly.

Today, I am on my way to America
because I am going to be adopted.

I have my suitcase ready. I don (put on) my chapeau (hat),
and I am ready to meet my new mommy and daddy.

When I arrive at the airport of Paris, the flight attendant,
Miss DiAnne, helps me find my seat.

Miss DiAnne straps me in,
and I put on my headphones
to listen to music.

I look up and see there is a movie showing.
I hope I can stay awake to watch it!

Before I know it, I am fast asleep. When I wake up, the plane has landed in Tennessee. I am finally in America!

WELCOME
COPPER

Miss DiAnne escorts me to where my new mommy and daddy are waiting. They are so excited to see me, and I am excited to see them, but I am also a little nervous. I begin to shake.

They hold me close and warm me with lots of hugs and kisses.

We ride in the automobile to my new maison (home) where I find lots of toys, good food, water, and my very own bed and blanket.

Wow! Being adopted is so nice.
I just know I am going to love it here!

My goodness, am I ever tired after that long flight. I think I will try
out my new bed and blanket and take a nice long nap,
but first, I must say my prayers.

Jesus, thank You for keeping me safe and bringing me to my new home and my wonderful new parents.
Amen.

AUTHOR'S NOTE

When God gave me the idea for a children's book some years ago, I never dreamed that our family would actually one day be involved in the adoption of a child!

Seven months ago, my daughter and son-in-law began the process of adoption—one they were told would take about two years to complete. Unbelievably, they are expecting a baby girl *this year*—about the time this book is to be published! Isn't our God an awesome God?

Sometimes I would become frustrated and discouraged by how long it was taking me to get my book together, but as always, God had a plan, and His timing is perfect.

It is my hope that this little story about Copper will help to make the transition easier for boys and girls who are being introduced to their new families and new homes.

Special thanks to Mary Harmon of ACT for the love and kindness she has shown our family throughout the entire adoption process.

Adoption Consultants in Tennessee, Inc. (ACT)
P. O. Box 50845
Knoxville, TN 37950
865-769-9441